D1523454

# COLORADO

## in words and pictures

**BY DENNIS B. FRADIN**

**ILLUSTRATIONS BY RICHARD WAHL**

**MAPS BY LEN W. MEENTS**

Consultant:
Dr. Marilee Bradbury
Elementary Social Studies Consultant
Jefferson County Public Schools
Lakewood

**CHILDRENS PRESS, CHICAGO**

*For my dear sister, Lori Fradin*

For his help, the author thanks:
Denny Davies, Chief of Interpretation
Dinosaur National Monument

Mount Elbert is the highest mountain in Colorado.

Library of Congress Cataloging in Publication Data

Fradin, Dennis B
Colorado in words and pictures.

SUMMARY: A brief introduction to the history of
the Centennial State and its geography, industries,
cities, major tourist attractions, and famous citizens.
1. Colorado—Juvenile literature. [1. Colorado]
I. Wahl, Richard, 1939-  II. Meents, Len W.
III. Title.
F776.F69        978.8        80-15778
ISBN 0-516-03906-7

*Picture Acknowledgments:*

JAMES P. ROWAN—Cover, pages 16, 19(right), 31 (top left and bottom),
37

TRAVEL MARKETING SECTION, STATE OF COLORADO. PHOTOS BY
STALEY STUDIO—pages 2, 11, 19(left), 21, 22, 31 (top right), 32

UNITED STATES DEPARTMENT OF THE INTERIOR, NATIONAL PARK
SERVICE, DINOSAUR NATIONAL MONUMENT—page 5

UNITED STATES DEPARTMENT OF THE INTERIOR, NATIONAL PARK
SERVICE, ROCKY MOUNTAIN REGIONAL OFFICE, DINOSAUR
NATIONAL MONUMENT—pages 38, 40

UNITED STATES DEPARTMENT OF THE INTERIOR, NATIONAL PARK
SERVICE, ROCKY MOUNTAIN REGIONAL OFFICE, ROCKY MOUNTAIN
NATIONAL PARK—pages 6, 42

UNITED STATES DEPARTMENT OF THE INTERIOR, NATIONAL PARK
SERVICE, ROCKY MOUNTAIN REGIONAL OFFICE, MESA VERDE
NATIONAL PARK—page 7

STEPHEN SCHWOCHOW, GOLDEN, COLORADO—pages 12, 14, 36

VAIL PHOTO BY PETER RUNYON—page 23

TRAVEL MARKETING SECTION, DIVISION OF COMMERCE AND
DEVELOPMENT, STATE OF COLORADO—page 25

NATIONAL BUREAU OF STANDARDS, UNITED STATES DEPARTMENT
OF COMMERCE—page 29(right)

COVER PHOTO—Rio Grande River, Rio Grande National Forest, South
Fork, Colorado

Colorado

*Colorado* (kahl • uh • RAD • oh) means "red" in Spanish. The Colorado River was given this name because it has a red color. The river flows through some red sandstone canyons. This red sandstone gives the river its color. Later, the state was also given the name Colorado.

Colorado has beautiful Rocky Mountain scenery. Miners once took gold and silver from the mountains. Today, many people go there to ski. The state also has flatlands. There farmers grow crops and cowboys care for cattle. Many products—including rocket ships—are made in Colorado's cities. The state has much more.

3

Where have dinosaur (DINE • ah • sore) bones been found near a town named Dinosaur? Where can you see "ghost towns" named Bonanza (buh • NAN • zuh) and Goldfield? Where is the United States Air Force Academy located? Where was the boxer Jack Dempsey born?

As you will learn, the answer to all these questions is: Colorado!

About 100 million years ago, many kinds of dinosaurs lived in Colorado. Brontosaurus (brahnt • uh • SORE • us) was there. The name means "Thunder Lizard." He was so big that his footsteps echoed like thunder off the hills. Yet Brontosaurus was a peaceful plant eater. Tyrannosaurus Rex (tuh • RAN • uh • sore • us RECKS) was there, too. His name means "King of the Dinosaurs." He ate other dinosaurs with his swordlike teeth.

A technician uncovers large bones of a Sauropod dinosaur at Dinosaur National Monument.

The last dinosaurs died long ago. But dinosaur bones and footprints have been found. You can see some of them at Dinosaur National Monument. Some dinosaur bones can also be seen in Colorado museums.

Nymph Lake in Rocky Mountain National Park

The dinosaurs began to die out. At about the same time, the Rocky Mountains were forming. The earth's surface cracked. Huge rocks rose on one side of the crack. The raised rocks became the Rocky Mountains. The Rockies are very young—for mountains. They were formed only about 70 million years ago.

The first people arrived in the area at least 20,000 years ago. Their stone tools and weapons have been found. It is thought that they hunted mammoths. Mammoths looked like big hairy elephants. Little is known about these early people.

More is known about the Basket Makers. They were Indians who lived in Colorado about 2,000 years ago. They wove baskets of branches and grasses. Clothes and sandals were woven that way, too. The Basket Makers learned to grow corn and squash. Farming meant they could stay in one place. They lived in caves at first. Later they learned how to build houses of branches and dirt.

About 1,000 years ago some Indians moved up into the mountains. There they were safer from wild animals and enemies. They built homes in mountain cliffs. These people are now remembered as the Cliff Dwellers. Cliff Dweller villages can still be seen at Mesa Verde (MAY • suh VUHRD) National Park.

Cliff Dweller ruins in Mesa Verde National Park

When white explorers arrived, a number of Indian tribes lived in the area. Eastern Colorado is a level plain. Millions of buffalo once grazed in this area. Cheyenne (shy • ANN), Comanche (kuh • MAN • chee), and Arapaho (uh • RAP • uh • ho) Indians hunted buffalo there. The Indians ate the buffalo meat. They made clothes from the buffalo skins. While hunting, the Indians lived in tents called tepees (TEE • peez).

The Ute (YOOT) Indians lived in the mountain valleys of the west. They hunted antelope (ANT • uhl • ope) and deer. They gathered berries and nuts. The Utes built cone-shaped houses. They were made of grass and reeds. To welcome spring, the Ute tribe held a Bear Dance. In the summer they held a Sun Dance. The Spanish brought horses to America in the 1500s. The Utes became fine horseback riders.

The Spanish were the first non-Indians in Colorado. In the 1500s and 1600s some Spaniards came to Colorado in search of gold.

In 1706 Spaniard Juan de Ulibarri (WAN day oo • lee • BAHR • ree) claimed Colorado for Spain. More Spaniards came to Colorado to look for gold. They did not find it. Most of the Spanish left the area. However, they still held claim to western Colorado. Eastern Colorado was claimed by France.

In the early 1800s American explorers came to Colorado. In 1806 Captain Zebulon M. Pike and some United States soldiers were sent from St. Louis to explore. At this time Americans knew almost nothing about Colorado. Pike and his soldiers wore summer clothes on their trip. They came to the Rocky Mountains in November. They nearly froze. Pike and his men saw a large mountain near present-day Pueblo (PWEB • loh). They tried to climb it, but couldn't. Pike said that no one would ever climb this mountain. It was later named Pikes Peak after him.

Pike and his men needed warm clothes. They made them from buffalo and beaver skins. They spent more time exploring the Colorado mountains and rivers. Later, they were captured by the Spanish. They spent about a year in a Spanish jail. Then they were released.

Longs Peak in Rocky Mountain National Park

In 1820 President Monroe sent Major Stephen Long to explore the Colorado area. Long reported that eastern Colorado was "a desert." He said nothing would grow there. Long also explored a mountain. It was named Longs Peak. You can see it in Rocky Mountain National Park. American fur trappers came to Colorado. They caught thousands of beavers and other animals. These furs were worth a lot of money. They could be made into fancy clothes.

A reconstruction of Bent's Old Fort, the first permanent American settlement in Colorado, can be seen near La Junta.

In 1833 a fort was built. It was meant to protect American fur trappers in Colorado. The fort was run by William Bent and three of his brothers. It was named Bent's Fort. Fort Bent was the first permanent American settlement in Colorado. You can see the rebuilt fort near La Junta (luh HOON • tuh).

Over the next few years a number of well-known American hunters and fur trappers entered Colorado. Jim Beckwourth, Kit Carson, and Jim Bridger are three of the names you may know. Beckwourth was a black man. He built a trading post called Fort Pueblo. It grew into the city of Pueblo. Kit Carson made maps of rivers in the area. He and another man once had a gunfight over an Indian woman. Carson won the fight, then married the woman. Jim Bridger was a fur trapper and hunter. He also explored the Rocky Mountains.

In 1803 the United States had bought eastern Colorado from France. The ownership of western Colorado passed from Spain to Mexico. The United States fought the Mexican War from 1846-1848. When this war ended, the United States took control of western Colorado. By 1848 all of Colorado belonged to the United States. It wasn't a state yet. It was land owned by the United States.

In 1858 gold was discovered in Colorado. It was found by a man named Green Russell. He found it at Cherry Creek, near the present city of Denver. Hundreds of people headed for Colorado. They were going into the area of Pikes Peak. They made signs that said PIKES PEAK OR BUST! This gold strike was very small. Many of the people ended up "busted."

On a cold January night in 1859 a man named George Jackson built a fire at Chicago Creek, also near Denver. Next to the fire he found gold dust. He also found a nugget of gold. This was the start of a large mine. In May of 1859 John Gregory made another huge gold find. That one was at nearby North Clear Creek.

Entrance (adit) to a tunnel at the site of the first Colorado gold rush in 1859

The news spread: "Gold! There's gold in Colorado!" In 1859 thousands came to Colorado to look for gold. The miners set up tents in the mountains. They went to the rivers and panned for gold. They chipped away the sides of hills to look for veins of gold. Most wound up with little or no gold. But some led their burros out of the mountains loaded with gold, or "pay dirt." Where gold was found, mines were built.

Some who didn't find gold set up stores in the mining camps. Miners traded gold dust for supplies at general stores. A pinch of gold dust was worth 25¢. A sack of potatoes cost $15.00 in those days. A five-pound bag of flour was more than $2.00. Eggs could be over $1.00 each. These supplies had to be sent a long distance by wagon to Colorado. At the camp saloons, miners drank whiskey. It was known as "Taos (TOUS) Lightning." Mining camps were wild places. Miners gambled for gold. There were fistfights. Sometimes there were gunfights.

Buckskin Joe, an early Colorado mining town
that became a ghost town

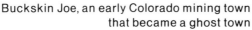

Some miners and storekeepers brought their families
to live in the mining camps. Houses were built. Soon the
camps had become towns. Buckskin Joe, Golden, Boulder
(BOLD • uhr), and Colorado City (later Colorado Springs)
were four of the towns built in the "gold rush" year of
1859. In that one year, about 100,000 Americans set out
for Colorado. Most of them were in search of gold. About
half of them reached the mining town of Denver City.
About a fourth, or 25,000, reached the gold camps in the
Rockies.

In 1861, the United States made Colorado a territory.

Most Indians had not been upset when only a few fur trappers were in the area. But thousands of people were arriving. The Indians were losing their lands. Miners climbed through mountains where Indians made their homes. They built towns where the Indians camped. Newcomers also killed millions of buffalo. Buffalo meat was an important food for many Indians. In anger, some Indians attacked wagon trains bringing supplies to Colorado. They attacked some settlements.

In October 1864, soldiers got revenge. A few hundred Cheyenne and Arapaho Indians had set up their tepees on Sand Creek. They were peaceful. To show this, they raised an American flag. Nonetheless, Colonel John Chivington attacked the Indian village. He had about 900 armed men. About 300 Indian men, women, and children were murdered. This tragic event is known as the Sand Creek Massacre (MASS • ih • kuhr). It was one of the bloodiest massacres in United States history.

The Indians in the region were enraged. In 1868 Cheyenne, Arapaho, and Sioux (SOO) Indians attacked about 50 soldiers on Beecher Island. It is in the Arikaree (ARE • ih • kahr • ee) River. Led by Chief Roman Nose, the Indians attacked again and again for a week. Finally, more soldiers arrived to save those on Beecher Island.

Fighting was over for a while. More settlers arrived. Colorado was ready to become a state. On August 1, 1876, Colorado became our thirty-eighth state. Denver was the capital. A "centennial" (sen • TEN • ee • uhl) marks the one hundredth year after an important event. The United States had been formed in 1776. Colorado became a state 100 years later. That is why it was nicknamed the *Centennial State.*

Gold mining became less important in the new state. Much of the gold was mined out. However, silver was found. Leadville and Aspen became important silver-mining towns. Later, in 1891, there was an important gold find at Cripple Creek.

Above: Cripple Creek was the site of a huge gold
find in 1891. Today, only a few hundred
people live here.
Left: You can take a trip into yesterday on
the Durango-Silverton train that runs
along the Navajo Trail.

In the 1870s gold and silver were found on Ute Indian
land. The United States government tried to force the
Utes out. In 1879, soldiers were sent onto Ute lands. The
Utes surrounded the soldiers at Milk Creek. A number of
soldiers were killed. The Indians also killed other white
people in what is called the "Meeker Massacre." After
this, Chief Ouray talked the Utes into making peace.
Most of the Utes were sent to Utah. Some were sent to a
small reservation in southwest Colorado. By 1879, most
of the fighting was over in Colorado.

During the 1880s huge cattle ranches were started on Colorado's eastern plains. Cowboys took care of the cattle herds. Trains were built through Colorado in the 1880s. The cattle were shipped from Colorado to eastern cities. The cattle were made into meat.

In the late 1880s more and more small farmers moved into the state. They built farmhouses. They fenced in the ranges. Large herds needed a lot of room. Without that room, the huge cattle ranches did not survive. However, cattle are still raised today on smaller ranches.

Farmers in eastern Colorado began to grow potatoes. They also grew sugar beets.

Colorado farmers had a big problem. In many areas there wasn't enough water. This was especially true in the east. Melting snow in the mountains created a lot of water. Rivers were filled with water. The farms needed this water. But there was no way to bring it where it was needed. In the 1930s long periods of dry weather made matters worse. There were dust storms.

Horsetooth Reservoir near Fort Collins

*Irrigation* means bringing water to dry places. Throughout the 1900s, a number of irrigation projects have been completed. Water is kept in large pools. They are called reservoirs (REZ • ehr • vwahrz). When water is needed, it is pumped through canals and tunnels to the thirsty land. The Alva B. Adams Tunnel was built in 1947. It takes water through the Rocky Mountains of western Colorado to dry areas in the east. Many dams have also been built. They help keep rivers from flooding. When the water is needed on farms, the dams release it.

Wheat is a major crop in the high plains of eastern Colorado.

You will remember that Stephen Long once called eastern Colorado "a desert." It might have been a desert, if there had not been irrigation. But today corn, wheat, sugar beets, and potatoes are just some of the crops grown in eastern Colorado. In recent years manufacturing has become important in Colorado. Manufacturing means making products in factories. It has become more important than farming. Rocket ships and space satellites have been made in the state. Food is packaged there. Denver, Pueblo, and Colorado Springs are main manufacturing centers. Denver is also Colorado's largest city.

Factories caused pollution, however. Colorado's air had been famous for being so clear. Now it was losing some clearness. Some streams were no longer clean. Colorado passed a number of conservation (kahn • suhr • VAY • shun) laws. These laws protect the air, land, and water.

Today, the word "Colorado" makes many people think of skiing. The Colorado Rockies get a lot of snow. The snow is light and powdery. It is perfect for skiing. Every year, thousands go to ski in such mountain areas as Aspen and Vail.

You have learned about some of Colorado's history. Now it is time for a trip—in words and pictures—through the Centennial State.

Skiing at Vail

Colorado is shaped like a rectangle. Wyoming (wye •
OH • ming) and Nebraska (neh • BRASS • kuh) are the
states to the north. Nebraska and Kansas (CAN • zuss)
are to the east. Oklahoma (oh • kluh • HO • mah) and New
Mexico (noo MEKS • ih • koh) are the states to the south.
Arizona (air • ah • ZONE • ah) touches the southwest
corner. Utah (YOU • taw) is to the west. Colorado is our
eighth largest state.

Pretend you are in an airplane high above Colorado. In
eastern Colorado you pass over long stretches of flat
land. Eastern Colorado is part of the Great Plains. Most
of the state's farms and ranches are in this area.

To the west, you can see the Rocky Mountains. They
rise up like a great wall. The Rockies make up much of
western Colorado. The state's biggest cities lie where the
Great Plains meet the Rocky Mountains. That is near the
middle of the state.

A view of Denver

Pretend your airplane is landing in Denver. It is the biggest city in the state—by far. Denver is also the capital of Colorado.

Once, Arapaho and Cheyenne Indians hunted in this area. Gold was found at nearby Cherry Creek in 1858. Denver was built as a place for miners to get supplies. The town was named after a governor of Kansas. His name was James W. Denver. Railroads brought even more people into Denver in the 1870s. Silver strikes in the area brought thousands in the 1880s. Today, about half the people in the whole state live in the Denver area.

The state capitol, Denver

Visit the state capitol building. The dome glitters with real gold. It was taken from the Colorado hills. Inside the capitol men and women make laws for the Centennial State. Denver is nicknamed the *Mile High City*. That is because the state capitol building is exactly 5,280 feet above sea level. A mile is 5,280 feet.

If you have some coins, look to see if they have a "D" on them. Those with a "D" were made in Denver. You will enjoy a trip to the United States Mint in Denver. This is the place where the coins are made.

Denver became home to the mint in 1906. Gold and silver found in the area made it a good place for making coins. Until 1931, some coins were made of gold. Today, the mint can make about a million coins an hour. You can watch how the coins are made.

Denver has some fine museums. At the Denver Museum of Natural History you can see dinosaur fossils. You can learn about the Cliff Dwellers at the Colorado Heritage Center. At the Denver Art Museum you can see great Indian artwork. Denver also has a fine symphony orchestra (SIM • fah • nee ORK • ess • trah).

If you like sports, you'll love Denver. In the fall you can watch the Denver Broncos play football. They play at Mile High Stadium. The Colorado Rockies are Denver's hockey team. The Nuggets are the basketball team.

You'll see Indians, blacks, Mexican Americans, and many other ethnic groups in Denver. Many of the city's people work at government jobs. Others work at packaging foods. Toys, rocket ships, space satellites (SAT • uhl • ites), beer, and luggage are some products made in the Denver area. Products go by train, truck, or jet to other cities in America.

After visiting the Mile High City, head 27 miles north to Boulder. Arapaho Indians once hunted in the area. Boulder was founded as a gold-mining town in 1859.

As you walk through Boulder you will see many young people. Boulder is the home of the University of Colorado. The University has a big telescope. With its clear mountain air, Colorado is a fine place to study the stars.

Mountains make Boulder a beautiful city. Flagstaff Mountain is nearby. A huge rock formation stands like a wall near Boulder. It is known as "the Flatirons." Some

Some of Boulder's drinking water comes from
Arapaho Glacier (above).
Right: These two atomic clocks keep time with an error
of less than three-millionths of a second in a year.

of the city's drinking water comes from the ice of nearby
Arapaho Glacier.

Visit the National Bureau of Standards in Boulder.
Does your clock ever run "fast" or "slow"? The most
accurate clock in the United States can be seen at the
National Bureau of Standards. It is an atomic clock. It is
accurate to about three-millionths of a second over a
whole year.

An aerial view of Colorado Springs

After spending some time in Boulder, go about 95 miles south. You will come to Colorado Springs. Like Denver and Boulder, the city lies at the edge of the Rocky Mountains. It was begun in 1859 by some gold hunters from Kansas. Later, it became a health resort. People came to the area to bathe in the mineral spring waters. Today, Colorado Springs is the state's second largest city.

Long ago, this gold-mining town had shoot-outs in the streets. Hearing aids, computer parts, and tools are some of the products made in Colorado Springs.

Above: The United States Air Force Academy chapel near Colorado Springs.
Left and top left: Strange-shaped red rocks in Garden of the Gods near Colorado Springs.

Visit the United States Air Force Academy. It is just north of the city. This is where air force officers are trained.

Colorado Springs is near some of Colorado's best scenery. Garden of the Gods is just west of the city. This isn't a flower garden. It's a group of strange-shaped red rocks.

Pikes Peak is America's most famous mountain.

Pikes Peak is also very near Colorado Springs. It is
14,110 feet high. It is not Colorado's highest mountain.
Mount Elbert (14,433 feet) is the highest. But Pikes
Peak is probably the most famous mountain in the
United States. You can see its snow-covered top from a
long way off.

Do you remember that Zebulon Pike said no one would
ever climb Pikes Peak? He was wrong. The first known
climb of Pikes Peak was in 1820. Today, you can drive to
the top. A railroad will also take you up. The Ute Indians
had a legend about this mountain. They believed that the
Great Spirit made it. They said he did it by pouring snow

and ice through a hole in the sky. Then the Great Spirit
came down to the mountain and created birds and
animals.

Have you ever sung "America the Beautiful"?
Katherine Lee Bates was climbing Pikes Peak when she
made up a poem. The poem became the words to
"America the Beautiful." Think of Pikes Peak the next
time you sing about "purple mountain majesties."

Near Pikes Peak there is a small town named Cripple
Creek. In 1891 a cowboy named Robert Womack made a
gold strike here. He sold his claim for $500. Then he
went to have fun in nearby saloons. Robert Womack died
a poor man in Colorado Springs. But the gold he found at
Cripple Creek was the start of huge gold mines. Over the
years, over $400 million in gold was taken from the
Cripple Creek mines. At one time, Cripple Creek was a
booming town with thousands of people. Today much of
the gold is gone. Only a few hundred people live in
Cripple Creek.

Near Colorado Springs there are a number of "ghost towns." Ghost towns have buildings. But most of them are empty. There are almost *no* people. The people left the towns when the gold was gone. Bonanza and Goldfield are two ghost towns near Colorado Springs.

About 44 miles south of Colorado Springs is a city that is very much alive. This is Pueblo. Indians once hunted in this area. In about 1840, Jim Beckwourth built a fur-trading post here. He named it Fort Pueblo. Pueblo is the Spanish word for "village."

Today, Pueblo is one of Colorado's main manufacturing cities. Steel, flour, and bricks are just three of the products made in Pueblo.

You will enjoy a visit to the El Pueblo Museum. There you can learn about the Indians and early settlers of Pueblo.

After seeing Pueblo, head west. Go into the Rocky Mountains. All about you there are snow-capped mountains.

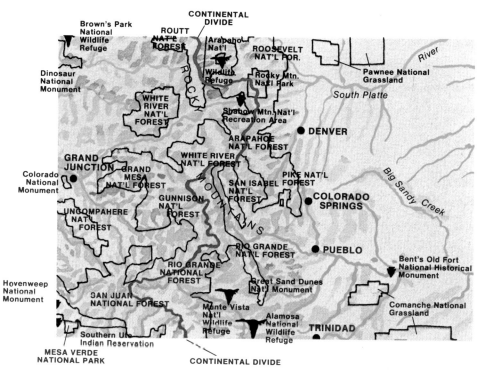

Colorado has at least 54 mountains over 14,000 feet high. They help make Colorado the highest of the 50 states. Some people like to hike through the mountains. In the winter, many like to ski. During the wintertime, you will see lots of snow in the mountains.

Some of the mountain areas have large forests of fir and pine trees. Many animals live in the forests and mountains. Nearly all the wolves that once lived there are gone. But there are still many bears. Mountain lions and bobcats prowl about. Deer and elk can be seen. Bighorn sheep like the highest places they can find. Beavers build their dams in mountain streams.

The Royal Gorge
suspension bridge

Rivers flow through the Rockies. Two of these are the Colorado and the Rio Grande. In some places, rivers have cut canyons through the rock. The Royal Gorge suspension (suh • SPEN • shun) bridge crosses one of these canyons. The bridge hangs 1,053 feet above the Arkansas (AR • kun • saw) River. It is the highest suspension bridge in the world.

Going west of Royal Gorge you will see signs. They say "CONTINENTAL DIVIDE." All rivers east of the Continental Divide flow into the Atlantic Ocean. The ones west of the Divide flow into the Pacific Ocean.

In the southwest corner of the state you will come to Mesa Verde National Park. A mesa is a hill with a flat top and steep sides.

The Cliff Palace in Mesa Verde National Park.

You can see Cliff Dweller houses in Mesa Verde National Park. The Cliff Dwellers built these houses about 1,000 years ago. One is the Cliff Palace. It is six stories high. It is thought that about 400 people lived inside. Scientists study the Cliff Dweller ruins. They work to find out what life was like here so long ago. They are also trying to find out why the Cliff Dwellers left their homes and where they went.

Very near Mesa Verde National Park is the Ute Mountain Indian Reservation. The Utes once hunted through vast areas. Now they live on this piece of land. Some of the Utes farm. Others work as teachers or at other jobs. In all, about 9,000 Indians still live in Colorado.

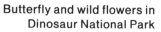
Butterfly and wild flowers in
Dinosaur National Park

Head up the straight western border of Colorado. You
will come to Dinosaur National Monument. It is near the
town of Dinosaur. It is in the northwest corner of the
state. Part of it extends into Utah. Many kinds of
dinosaur fossils have been found here. You could find
some fossils there.

You will see oil wells near Dinosaur National
Monument. Today, oil is Colorado's most important
mining product.

Head east from Dinosaur National Monument. Stop
for a visit at Rocky Mountain National Park. It contains
some of the loveliest scenery of the Rockies. You will see
mountains. One of these is Longs Peak. You will also see
lakes, meadows, and canyons in the park. Wild flowers
grow on the mountainsides. On some mountains there are
glaciers of ice. People aren't the only ones who enjoy the
park. Black bears, elk, and deer also live there.

Greeley is just about 40 miles east of Rocky Mountain National Park. Horace C. Greeley was a newspaperman. He helped found this town in 1870. Horace Greeley is famous for saying: "Go West, young man!" He felt that there was a good future for Americans out West in places like Colorado.

You're not going west, though! You're going into eastern Colorado. Here you will finish up your trip. Many people think Colorado has only the Rocky Mountains. But in eastern Colorado you will see long stretches of flat land. You will see cattle ranches.

You will see many farms where crops are grown. Wheat, corn, and sugar beets are important farm crops.

Cattle ranching in the Wet Mountain Valley of Custer County. The majestic Sangre de Cristo Range towers in the background.

A prairie dog looks out of his burrow.

Eastern Colorado has interesting animal life. You will see antelope (ANT • uh • lope) on the plains. Coyote (kye • OH • tee) live there. There are some rattlesnakes. Prairie dogs can also be seen. Prairie dogs are really a kind of squirrel. They dig large burrows in the ground. They build underground "rooms" for sleeping and storing food.

Places can't tell the whole story of Colorado. Many interesting people have lived in the Centennial State.

Horace A.W. Tabor was born in Vermont. But he went to Colorado. He was a miner. In the 1880s Tabor made millions of dollars. He became known as the "Silver King."

Enos Mills was born in Kansas in 1870. He moved to Colorado. He built a log cabin near Longs Peak. Mills thought this would be a good camping area. People could learn about wildlife. Mills wrote books about the area. He helped create Rocky Mountain National Park there.

Lon Chaney (CHAIN • ee) was born in Colorado Springs in 1883. Chaney became famous for playing many movie monsters. He could look scary so many ways that he was called the "man of a thousand faces."

Jack Dempsey was born in Manassa in 1895. Dempsey became one of the best heavyweight boxers ever. He was world heavyweight champion from 1919 to 1926. Dempsey was called the "Manassa Mauler."

Malcolm Scott Carpenter was born in Boulder in 1925. Scott Carpenter became a navy pilot. Later, he became an astronaut. In 1962 Carpenter became the second American to go around the earth in a space ship.

Eugene Fodor was born in 1950 in Turkey Creek. He became a violinist. When he was just eleven years old, Fodor played with the Denver Symphony. He became a very well-known violinist as an adult.

Rocky Mountain National Park scenery

Home to the Cliff Dwellers ... the Ute Indians ...
trappers ... and gold miners.

The beautiful land of Pikes Peak ... Mesa Verde ...
and the Royal Gorge.

A state where you can see Cliff Dweller Ruins ...
ghost towns ... the Mile High City ... and the United
States Mint.

A lovely land where bears, deer, and mountain lions
still roam.

Home of Ouray ... Lon Chaney ... and the "Manassa
Mauler."

This is Colorado—the Centennial State.

## Facts About COLORADO

Area—104,247 square miles (8th biggest state)

Greatest Distance East to West—387 miles

Greatest Distance North to South—276 miles

Border States—Wyoming and Nebraska on the north; Nebraska and Kansas on the east; Oklahoma and New Mexico on the south; Arizona touching the southwest corner; Utah on the west

Highest Point—14,433 feet above sea level (Mount Elbert)

Lowest Point—3,350 feet above sea level (on the Arkansas River)

Hottest Recorded Temperature—118°F. (at Bennett on July 11, 1888)

Coldest Recorded Temperature—Minus 60°F. (at Taylor Park Dam on February 1, 1951)

Statehood—Our 38th state, on August 1, 1876

Origin of Name Colorado—Colorado (meaning "red" or "ruddy" in Spanish) was the name given to the Colorado River; the state was given this name, too.

Capital—Denver (made capital in 1867 while Colorado was still a territory).

Previous Capitals—Colorado City (now the city of Colorado Springs) and Golden

Counties—63

U.S. Senators—2

U.S. Representatives—6

Electoral Votes—8

State Senators—35

State Representatives—65

State Song—"Where the Columbines Grow," by A.J. Flynn

State Motto—*Nil sine Numine* (Latin meaning "Nothing without Providence")

Nicknames—The Centennial State, the Highest State

State Seal—Adopted in 1877

State Flag—Adopted in 1911

State Flower—Rocky Mountain columbine

State Bird—Lark Bunting

State Animal—Rocky Mountain bighorn sheep

State Gemstone—Aquamarine

State Tree—Colorado blue spruce

State Colors—Blue and white

Some Rivers—Colorado, Arkansas, South Platte, Rio Grande, Republican, North Platte, Yampa, White, Dolores, Gunnison, Roaring Fork, San Juan

Largest Natural Lake—Grand Lake

Mountains—Rocky Mountains (made up of a number of ranges)

National Parks—2 (Mesa Verde National Park and Rocky Mountain National Park)

National Forests—12

Animals—Deer, black and brown bears, elk, pronghorn antelope, bighorn
   sheep, beavers, foxes, bobcats, mountain lions, martens, weasels, coyotes,
   porcupines, mink, muskrats, bats, pheasants, quail, eagles, woodpeckers,
   Rocky Mountain jays, road runners, many other kinds of birds, rattlesnakes,
   black widow spiders, tarantulas

Fishing—Perch, bass, trout, catfish

Farm Products—Beef cattle, milk, wheat, corn, sugar beets, beans, potatoes,
   onions, sheep, poultry, barley, melons, cherries, peaches, pears

Mining—Oil, molybdenum, coal, natural gas, limestone, uranium ore, gold,
   silver

Manufacturing Products—Suger, beer, and many other processed foods,
   rocket ships, space satellites and other space equipment, computer parts,
   tools, plastics, electrical machinery, scientific instruments, sports
   equipment, photographic equipment, steel

Population—2,888,834 (1980 census)

Major Cities—Denver                    491,396
             Colorado Springs          215,150
             Aurora                    158,588
             Lakewood                  112,848
             Pueblo                    101,686
             Arvada                     84,576
             Boulder                    76,685

## Colorado History

Tools and weapons of people who lived in Colorado at least 20,000 years ago
have been found. About 2,000 years ago Indians known as the Basket Makers
lived in Colorado. Indians known as the Cliff Dwellers lived at Mesa Verde
about 1,000 years ago.

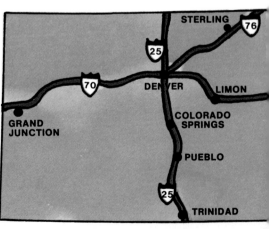

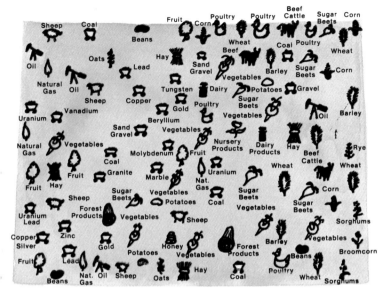

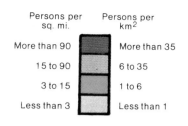

Persons per sq. mi. | Persons per km²
More than 90 | More than 35
15 to 90 | 6 to 35
3 to 15 | 1 to 6
Less than 3 | Less than 1

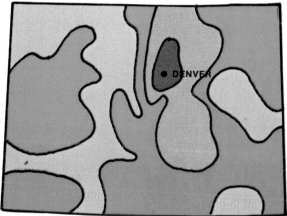

1066 — The Cliff Dwellers begin building the Cliff Palace about this year

1598 — The Spaniard Juan de Onate, hunting for gold, probably enters what is now Colorado

1682 — La Salle claims area of Colorado east of the Rocky Mountains for France

1706 — Juan de Ulibarri claims Colorado for Spain

1761 — Spaniard Juan Maria Rivera hunts for gold and silver in Colorado

1776 — Escalante and Dominguez explore Mesa Verde; in this same year United States is formed

1803 — United States buys Colorado land east of the Rocky Mountains from France (part of Louisiana Purchase)

1806 — American Zebulon M. Pike explores Colorado and tries to climb the mountain now bearing his name

1820 — American Stephen H. Long explores Colorado; a man with him, Dr. Edwin James, leads the first recorded climb up Pikes Peak

1821 — Mexico takes control of western Colorado from Spain

1833 — Bent's Fort — first permanent American settlement in Colorado — is built

1848 — The United States takes control of western Colorado from Mexico; the United States now controls all of Colorado

1858 — Gold is found at Cherry Creek; Denver is founded nearby

1859 — Gold rush to Colorado as gold is found at several places

1861 — Colorado Territory is created

1864 — Soldiers kill hundreds of Indians in Sand Creek Massacre

1867 — Denver becomes capital of the Colorado Territory

1868 — Indians battle soldiers at Beecher Island

45

1870—Population of Colorado Territory is 39,864; railroad is built to Denver, making it easier to get to Colorado

1873—Some of the Utes' land is taken from them by treaty

1876—On August 1, Colorado becomes the 38th state; Denver is the capital

1877—University of Colorado opens at Boulder

1878—Big silver strikes in Colorado

1879—Ute Indians battle soldiers, then kill other people on their lands in the "Meeker Massacre"; Chief Ouray has his people make peace, ending fighting in Colorado

1880—Population of Colorado is 194,327; this year Chief Ouray dies

1881—Most of Ute Indians are forced into Utah

1891—Robert Womack makes big gold find at Cripple Creek; he sells claim for $500 and it becomes one of the world's greatest gold-mining areas

1893—Colorado is second state to allow women to vote (Wyoming was the first)

1900—Population of Colorado is 539,700

1906—The United States Mint at Denver makes its first coins; in this same year Mesa Verde National Park is created

1914-1918—During World War I, about 43,000 Coloradoans are in uniform

1915—Rocky Mountain National Park is created

1921—Huge flood at Pueblo

1927—Moffat Tunnel, allowing trains to go through the Rocky Mountains, is finished

1929—Royal Gorge suspension bridge (highest suspension bridge in the world) opens

1932-1937—Dry weather and dust storms hurt farming in eastern Colorado

1939-1945—During World War II, 138,832 Coloradoans serve

1947—Alva B. Adams Tunnel, carrying water from western to eastern Colorado, is completed

1954—National Bureau of Standards moves to Boulder

1956—Work begins on irrigation program known as the Colorado River Storage Project

1958—United States Air Force Academy opens near Colorado Springs

1959—Irrigation project known as the Colorado-Big Thompson Project is completed

1962—Astronaut Malcolm Scott Carpenter, born in Boulder, becomes the second American to orbit the Earth

1963—North American Air Defense Command (NORAD) is established near Colorado Springs

1967—Frying Pan-Arkansas River Project, an irrigation project to bring water to eastern Colorado, is begun

1970—Population of Centennial State is 2,207,259

1976—Happy 100th birthday, Centennial State! In this year there is a large flood of the Big Thompson River

1977—Denver Broncos are in Super Bowl of football, but lose

1978—Richard D. Lamm is elected to second term as governor

1982—Richard D. Lamm is elected to third term as governor

# INDEX

## INDEX, Cont'd

About the Author:

Dennis Fradin attended Northwestern University on a creative writing scholarship and graduated in 1967. While still at Northwestern, he published his first stories in *Ingenue* magazine and also won a prize in *Seventeen's* short story competition. A prolific writer, Dennis Fradin has been regularly publishing stories in such diverse places as *The Saturday Evening Post, Scholastic, National Humane Review, Midwest,* and *The Teaching Paper.* He has also scripted several educational films. Since 1970 he has taught second grade reading in a Chicago school—a rewarding job, which, the author says, "provides a captive audience on whom I test my children's stories." Married and the father of three children, Dennis Fradin spends his free time with his family or playing a myriad of sports and games with his childhood chums.

About the Artists:

Len Meents studied painting and drawing at Southern Illinois University and after graduation in 1969 he moved to Chicago. Mr. Meents works full time as a painter and illustrator. He and his wife and child currently make their home in LaGrange, Illinois.

Richard Wahl, graduate of the Art Center College of Design in Los Angeles, has illustrated a number of magazine articles and booklets. He is a skilled artist and photographer who advocates realistic interpretations of his subjects. He lives with his wife and two sons in Libertyville, Illinois.